take care of the

DIFFICULT

TODAY

and leave the

IMPOSSIBLE

FOR TOMORROW

feb 29:11

MARY E. BARRERAS

take care of the

DIFFICULT

TODAY

and leave the

IMPOSSIBLE

FOR TOMORROW

TATE PUBLISHING & *Enterprises*

Published by Tate Publishing & Enterprises, LLC
127 E. Trade Center Terrace | Mustang, Oklahoma 73064 USA
1.888.361.9473 | www.tatepublishing.com

Tate Publishing is committed to excellence in the publishing industry. The company reflects the philosophy established by the founders, based on Psalm 68:11,
"The Lord gave the word and great was the company of those who published it."

Book design copyright © 2010 by Tate Publishing, LLC. All rights reserved.
Cover design by Lauran Levy
Interior design by Blake Brasor

Published in the United States of America

ISBN: 978-1-61739-272-6
1. Religion, Christian Life, Inspirational
2. Self-Help, Spiritual
10.10.06

Dedication

To a woman who I love, admire, and appreciate so very much, my loving sister-in-law and friend, Vicki Everhart. You have always been a great encourager and have always been there for me, and I thank God for you. You have been on the battlefield the last two years fighting breast cancer and you have fought well. You are experiencing victories each day and slowly regaining strength, and you have still found time to reach out to others and encourage them. You are a rock to many people, and I can only hope that I can be a rock for you. I love you with an everlasting love, and I will always be grateful to God for putting you in my life.

Acknowledgments

Words cannot express my deep gratefulness for the loving support I have received from my husband, Dennis, and children, who generously shared me with this manuscript. I appreciate and love you all so much. A big thank you to Dr. Donald Kwasman; this book would never have been written if you had not shared with me what your father shared with you so many times: "Take care of the difficult things today. Leave the impossible things for tomorrow." Those words blessed me very much and have helped me get through the storm. Thank you to Vicki Everhart, who tirelessly labored to enhance this project with her insights and creativity and hours of proofreading and editing.

Table of Contents

Foreword

When my son, Adam, was about eight years old, I remember him asking me, "Daddy, how many people have you healed since you became a doctor?"

I answered him with a question, "By myself?"

He said, "Yes."

I answered, "Zero. I have never healed anybody without God's help."

Adam smiled and said before leaving the room and helping his mother with dinner, "That's a pretty big helper, Dad!"

I couldn't help thinking to myself, *I know, and that's why I've been blessed the way I have.*

My thirty years of medical practice in southern Arizona has seen tens of thousands of success stories and the rise of a family of patients in Tucson that has struggled together and healed together. My focus on wellness and prevention has been inspired by heeding God's voice in Deuteronomy 4:15, "You shall be exceedingly careful regarding your being." This statement is a sweeping commandment to take care of our bodies and ourselves. The fact that God commanded us to be exceedingly careful regarding our being as he spoke about the dietary laws of Israel brings a distinct linkage that cannot be overemphasized in our modern American world. Our eating habits and our lifestyles must be looked after as a *holy task.*

As Mary and I began to work together, I noticed that she wore a Star of David around her neck. The star, for her, represents the relationship she has with God. Interestingly, in Hebrew, the Star of David translates into *Magen David*, literally meaning the "shield" of David, who is, of course, God almighty. I know in my heart that God truly shields Mary and has been an intricate part of her successes. While working with her, Mary immediately understood that being healthy is a lifestyle. It is a holistic approach in the very essence of the word. Success must come from not only changing your physical approach to life but changing your spiritual being as well. Mary's relationship with God is an inspiration to me, and I hope Mary's story will be able to help you improve your life. In this book, Mary provides us with inspiration and knowledge that our lives have a higher purpose, and we can achieve any goal if we take the time to recognize that God is standing there right along side of us.

Remember: take care of the difficult things today; leave the impossible things for tomorrow.

Donald L. Kwasman D.O.

Introduction

"Take care of the difficult things today. Leave the impossible things for tomorrow."

These are the words that my doctor told me during a recent visit. Although he has been my family doctor on and off for the last twenty years, for more than a year I had been seeing Dr. Kwasman as I battled a weight problem. In January 2008, my husband and I decided we both needed to get healthy. We were both overweight, and we both had medical problems. I had already lost thirty pounds, but I had reached that common plateau and had stopped losing, so I went for help. In April of 2009 when I went for my doctor visit, it had been more than four months since I had lost any weight and I was very discouraged. Well, I would lose two pounds and then gain two pounds, but that was hardly progress. Needless to say, my doctor was not any happier about my lack of progress than I was and told me, "It's time that you buck up and buckle down." Then he said something so profound that it really struck a chord with me. He told me that I needed to "take care of the difficult things today and leave the impossible things for tomorrow." He said his father had imparted those words of wisdom so many times and they had always helped him. It made me think of the scripture that says, "Therefore do not worry about tomorrow, for tomorrow will worry about its own things. Sufficient for the day is its own trouble" (Matthew 6:34 NKJV). On that particular day, it was also just what I needed to hear. In those fateful words of encouragement from my doctor, this book was conceived. I have always had a strong faith and always looked to God for guidance. Don't mistake my strong faith for having an easy life. We all know that it's easy to be strong and easy to shout your faith from the rooftops when life is going smoothly, but I can assure you that my faith has been tested over and over through the years. Although I have endured many, many difficulties, I have been able to persevere and survive the troubled times because of my faith and strong belief in God.

God has spoken to my heart in a multitude of ways over the years. He has promised that he is with us through the good times and the difficult times. What more difficult times than those our world faces today? Families are struggling as never before, not only with the economic and political issues but also with spiritual and personal burdens. I read a quote once that said, "God doesn't promise security from life's storms, but security in life's storms." Life is not easy, but I am hopeful that the messages and practical applications contained in this book will help to ease the difficult journeys of those who read it and put the messages to use in their own lives. In short, my counsel to you is simple: Take care of the difficult things today; give the impossible things to God.

My First God Encounter

I love the Lord, because He has heard my voice and
my supplications, Because He has inclined His ear to
me, Therefore I will call upon Him as long as I live.
Psalm 116:1–2 (NKJV)

I was born into a life of hardship and difficulty. I was the
seventh child of eight, and my father died of cancer when
I was three, leaving my uneducated and struggling mom
to raise us alone. We lived in poverty, yet we were very
rich. I say rich because my mother, Ruth, taught us how
to pray as soon as we could talk. We were raised attending
church every Sunday and Wednesday, and every night if
there was a revival in town. As a small child, my mother
would take me to the altar every Sunday to pray. She never
taught me a certain prayer to say; she just let me know
that talking to God was praying and encouraged us to be
prayerful in all that we did. Mom also taught me that God
was now our Father, who would take care of us and keep
us together. When we were sick, she didn't call the doctor, because there just wasn't money for that or insurance.
Instead, it was the pastor she called to come over to pray
for us. When we were in need, it was God that she called
on to supply our needs. I was very blessed to have learned
the Scriptures and to pray at an early age. My mother

taught me how to have faith in God, and I will forever be grateful to her for that.

My mother worked from early morning to late at night, so we were sometimes left to take care of ourselves, and although socially acceptable in those days, it sometimes put us in danger. At the age of nine, I went through a particularly difficult time. A relative, who was in his late thirties, started sexually abusing me. He was a very violent person, and having witnessed him losing control of his temper many times and beating people up, I was very afraid of him and took his threats seriously. I was very afraid to tell anyone and felt like I had no one to turn to or confide in.

It was the summer of 1969. On a typical day, my mom would leave early in the morning to go to work; my brothers would take off to their friends' houses; and my sister had a summer babysitting job. I was alone and vulnerable, a fact that my abuser knew and took advantage of. At the tender age of nine, I wanted to die. My body hurt from the abuse, and I was tired. I had a terrible secret that I could not tell anyone because of the fear my abuser had instilled in me, a fear of me or my family being beaten or killed. I often entertained the thought, *I could run away. Maybe someone will let me live with them and I can cook and clean for them.* Of course, as frightened as I was to stay, I was equally frightened to run away and face the fear of not being able to find someone else to live with to protect me. What if someone didn't let me live with them, then what would I do?

At nine years old, I was a little girl in a situation no child should ever be in, living in fear, not knowing what was going to happen to me next and so very alone in my secret. I began to think, *If God is my father maybe I should go talk to him about my problem.* I had loved God from the time I can remember, and I recalled the stories I learned in church, how God helped David kill the Giant, how God did not let the three Hebrew boys, Shadrach, Meshach, and Abednego burn while they were in the fiery furnace, and how God protected Daniel in the Lion's den. *Surely if God did these things for those people in the Bible, he could help me, if only he loved me like he loved them.* That was the question in my mind: *Did he love me just as much? Will he be a father to me or is my mom just telling me that?*

An important turning point for me was a day that started like so many others. My sister and I shared a bedroom upstairs in our big two-story house; we had a very small closet in our room. That closet became my safe haven, and I would go there often to hide, to be alone, and to talk to God at times; and it was the place I felt the safest. On the day I made a conscious decision to talk to God about my secret, I had just been abused. I went into my closet with the weight of the world on my little shoulders to share something with God that I had told no one, hoping that he would be able to help me. My mother had taught me that prayer was the most powerful thing in the world. On this fateful day, I was hoping she was right. I began to cry out to God as a child who was being hurt would cry out to their father. I told him what was happening to me and I told him, "My mom told me you're my father. I need you to help me. Please, please help me." In sad desperation, I told God, "If you don't help me, then please just let me die." I meant it. I was crying out with all that was within me. I'm not sure how long I was in my closet that day, but it seemed like an eternity. Suddenly,

I felt these huge arms around me. I did not see anyone, and there was not enough room in my tiny closet for anyone else. I knew instantly that God was in my small bedroom closet. I didn't see him. He didn't say anything, but in that moment, I felt his strong, loving, and protective arms around me, and I knew with my whole heart that he was there. A supernatural peace like none I have ever known filled me, soothing my broken heart and spirit. I felt warm and safe. I felt loved. God was rocking me in his arms. I don't remember ever being rocked before, but I had often daydreamed about having a father that would rock me and care for me. Now I was in the arms of God almighty. I went into my closet that day feeling shamed, dirty, afraid, and all alone, but I came out knowing that God loved me, was going to take care of me, and I could trust him.

I know a lot of preachers who say, "We don't live by feelings but by faith," but it is especially comforting when you feel God. After that profound experience in my closet, God started speaking to me through my dreams. I would dream of my abuser coming and I heard a voice in the dream that would tell me where to go to hide and what time I needed to hide. I soon realized that this was how God was speaking to me to protect me from my abuser. On one occasion, my dream showed me to hide in our basement, under the stairwell, while another dream showed me to hide in the linen closet. Each time I acted on what the dream told me, and each time I would hear my abuser coming, calling out my name. I was scared and my heart beat so fast and so loudly that I just knew he was going to hear it, but he didn't. Because I was able to avoid him through God's direction, I was never abused by him again. Soon after, he was arrested for abusing someone else, and ended up in the state mental hospital, where he was kept until he died from a brain disease. I never saw him again, but I never forgot how God had protected me.

Some would question why God would allow abuse to happen in the first place. All I can say is that God has given everyone a free will and some choose to do evil with their free will. But that experience caused me to have a strong trust in God at a very young age. I trusted God to be a father to me. It gave me knowledge and comfort that if I go to him, he is faithful to take care of my needs. He has been and is a loving Father, friend, and Lord to me. I allowed God to take care of what was impossible for me to take care of alone. The difficult thing for me then and sometimes now, was to go to God with my burden instead of trying to fix things myself. There are times when we don't even think of going to God. We try to take care of things ourselves, but he is waiting patiently for us to call upon him. "Casting all your care upon Him, because He cares for you" (1 Peter 5:7, NKJV).

When we truly believe that God cares for us, is when we will begin to trust God enough to go to him with all our cares, our anxieties, and our worries.

We Have Choices—We Have Free Will

I call heaven and earth as witnesses today against
you, that I have set before you life and death, blessing
and cursing; therefore choose life, that both you and
your descendants may live.

Deuteronomy 30:19 (NKJV)

It is not easy giving things over to God; it is a difficult
thing, so difficult that many times we choose not to. When
we don't let God take care of the impossible and we direct
our energy and worry on the impossible things that are
out of our control, then successfully handling the difficult
things in life is simply not going to happen. When we
don't take care of the difficult things in life, they will begin
to build up and sometimes become the impossible things.
When we worry about our tomorrows, it will hinder us
from doing the things that need to get done today.

To successfully take care of the difficult things, our
first step is to determine what those things are. Usually
they are the things we would rather not face, the things
we want to put off until tomorrow because they are difficult, but that tomorrow never comes. What are the difficult things you are facing in your life?

- Maybe your spending habits are out of control, leaving you overwhelmed by debt.
- Maybe you need to forgive someone for a hurt that threatens to turn into bitterness.
- Maybe you are full of an uncontrollable anger whose source you no longer remember.
- Maybe your home life is chaotic, out of control, and in need of direction.
- Maybe you are facing the impending death of a loved one and are having difficulty dealing with the emotional and planning needs.
- Maybe you are the caregiver of a parent or other loved one and find yourself overwhelmed.
- Maybe you have health issues and know you need to take steps now, so you can live longer and have a better life.
- Maybe you need to renew your relationship with God and let him become important in your life again.

There are so many things life brings to us, and with them we have choices to make. Sometimes we make the wrong choices and life becomes more difficult, and then there are the times we allow God to help us; we make some right choices and we grow from the difficulties in our life. We can either grow from the storms of life, or we can become beaten down and broken from life's difficulties. We can become bitter or we can become better.

I have always found answers in the Word of God to help me with life's difficulties. There are people who believe that the Bible is outdated. They say it really does not apply to modern times, but I have found that the Scriptures help me and bless me, both during the good times and the bad times, whether they are from the Hebrew Scriptures or the New Testament. Proverbs speaks extensively about wisdom; I believe we live in an age that lacks wisdom, a time when it's easier or more convenient for men to choose not to apply the wisdom of the Bible to their everyday lives.

> My son, if you receive My Words, and treasure My commands within you, So that you incline your ear to wisdom, and apply your heart to understanding; Yes, if you cry out for discernment, and lift up your voice for understanding, If you seek her as silver, and search for her as for hidden treasures; Then you will understand the fear of the Lord, and find the knowledge of God. For the Lord gives wisdom; From His mouth come knowledge and understanding; He stores up sound wisdom for the upright; He is a shield to those who walk uprightly; He guards the paths of justice, and preserves the way of His saints. Then you will understand righteousness and justice, equity and every good path. When wisdom enters your heart and knowledge is pleasant to your soul. Discretion will preserve you; Understanding will keep you, to deliver you from the way of evil, from the man who speaks perverse things.
>
> Proverbs 2:1–12 (NKJV)

There are three "Ifs" here:

1) If you receive My words
2) If you cry out for discernment
3) If you seek her (wisdom) as silver

The promises, if we do these three things, are that we will understand the fear of the Lord, which is the foundation to a walk of faith, the fear of the Lord means to honor him, to reverence God, to be in awe of God's majesty, his holiness, his sovereign grace. Walking in the fear of the Lord will bring a life of fulfillment; people who don't receive God's Word do not understand the fear of God and what it means. God says if we do these three things, we will find his knowledge; we will receive wisdom from the Lord. God said he will be our shield and he will guard our path and preserve our way. In addition, we will understand righteousness and justice; we will gain wisdom, discretion, and understanding. There are many people with book knowledge, degrees upon degrees, but they have no wisdom or discretion whatsoever. God desires to give us wisdom, but we must seek it. When you want something bad enough, you will work for it. When we allow wisdom to enter our heart, discretion will become second nature. We will recognize and acknowledge boundaries. We will know which people to allow in our life and which people with whom to maintain strong boundaries. Applying wisdom to our everyday life will help us through the difficulties, and it will alleviate many self-induced hardships. Judges 13 through 16 in the Hebrew Scriptures tells the story about Samson, just one of many examples in the Bible about choices and free will. He was a man who rejected wisdom. He was the son of Manoah. Samson was a Nazarite, separated and consecrated unto God. Being a Nazarite, Samson could not cut his hair, touch a dead body, or drink anything containing alcohol. Yet, as with many people today, he chose to involve himself with evil associations, and he was influenced by the wrong people. Samson was mighty in physical strength yet weak in resisting the temptation that brought a sad end to his life. Samson was born and destined to deliver Israel out of the hand of the Philistines. God had a purpose for his life, as he does for everyone who is born. As you read his story, you will see where Samson violated his vows and God's laws on many occasions. He allowed his lust to control him. He did not value the gifts that God gave him and used the gifts that God gave him unwisely, trusting and confiding in the wrong people. It was God's strength that was imbued in Samson, but Samson became filled with self-importance and boasted of his own strength. Because of his bad choices, he ended up in the hands of the Philistines.

There are times when we forget that the gifts we have come from God, and we use our gifts for the wrong reasons. We fail to give God the glory, and we selfishly want the credit for what God has done for us. We choose to follow our own path; we don't want to accept wise counsel. And then when we fail, we want to blame God. Some even curse God. In our ministry, my husband and I work with people who have a background of drug and alcohol addictions. Many times, these same people can't get a job, or they have lost their children or alienated their families and friends. They usually have few material possessions. They have burned many bridges behind them, so not many people want to help them out. These same people will ask, "Why did God give me this life?" They don't see or take ownership of the fact that it was their own choices that put them where they are. I'm not trying to assign guilt or point fingers, but until we face our wrongs, our poor choices, we won't be able to make them right. As long as we put the blame on God or somebody else, things will never get corrected in our life. The best part is that our loving and forgiving Savior allows U-turns when we decide to do something about our messes. It takes a commitment to make a life change to bring about a truly successful U-turn. We do see that when Samson calls on God one more time that God heard his cry. In the end, Samson recognized his dependence on God. God turned Samson's failures into victory, and Samson was able to deliver the people of Israel from the Philistines. Samson made that U-turn to some degree, but it was not without a price. While God still used Samson to deliver Israel, Samson died with the Philistines. Samson's eyes were gouged out, and he lived the last part of his life defeated. It was not the plan God had for him, but it was the life Samson chose by choosing foolishness instead of wisdom. The wise choices may not always seem as fulfilling at the time, and they may not seem too fun, but they will keep us on the right path. We face choices every day, and there are times that the hard thing is the right thing to do. It is up to us to make those choices.

Choose to be Healthy

Beloved, I pray that you may prosper in all things and be in health, just as your soul prospers.

3 John 2 (NKJV)

When we are being held back from doing the things we need to do, it is time to take a good look at ourselves, and that's exactly what my husband and I realized that we needed to do! We had neglected our personal health for far too long. We got tired easily, and we did not have the energy that we needed. He had high cholesterol, high blood pressure, and thyroid problems, and was overweight. I suffered from type 2 diabetes, thyroid problems, and was also overweight. Health problems affect us all, either through personal health issues or through someone we care about. A young man came for counseling whose father died at age fifty-two. This young man was mad at God for taking his father. In counseling with him, we reminded him that his father's health problems and subsequent death were a result of his failure to take care of his health and not necessarily because it was God's will that he should die. His father was an alcoholic and a drug addict on top of the health problems. The choices his father made harmed his health even more.

My childhood pastor, Fred Hill, now a young-looking and energetic eighty-year-old, came to preach as a guest minister in our church last year. My husband and I were immediately struck by the high level of energy exhibited by Pastor Hill and his seventy-five-year-old wife, Betty. Seeing their vibrant health firsthand was a true wake-up call for both me and my husband. It was just what we needed to spur us to decide to do something about our own lax health habits. When health problems are due to poor choices, you can choose life instead of death by adopting a healthy lifestyle. With perseverance and commitment to our new healthy way of living, I have now lost ninety pounds, and my husband has lost forty pounds. It has not been easy, but we are committed to losing down to a healthy weight. Those results are also reflected in our medications. I have been able to lower my medication by a whopping 80 percent, and I hope to soon no longer need it at all.

What did we do to lose weight and get healthy? We did not go on a diet. Diets will help you lose weight initially, but it takes a lifestyle change and commitment to keep the weight off. That lifestyle change is not just about the food consumed; it's also about making time every day to exercise and making it a way of life. If you truly make a commitment to a healthier lifestyle and truly want to make changes in your life, you will find time to plan good nutritious meals, make healthy choices, and increase your activity level.

Are you ready to make that commitment to a healthy lifestyle but don't know where or how to start? The first step is to identify your health problems and then make a plan to address the issues you are facing. If you are overweight, then it's important to identify why. Obesity can be caused by eating too much or by eating the wrong things.

If you are turning to food for comfort or when you are stressed, then you need to make an honest assessment to determine what is missing in your life and what is causing your stress that makes you turn to food for comfort. Is food your addiction? When did it become your addiction? Who can you go to for help? Deciding to do something about it and making a commitment to change is the first step in recovery of any addiction, including a food addiction.

For myself, I can honestly say that eating too much has never been my problem. Sometimes I will even forget about eating when I am busy. I don't think about food that much. However, eating the wrong foods and eating fast food too frequently, along with some other health issues, has caused my weight problems. At age fifteen I was diagnosed with thyroid problems and borderline diabetes. The health problems did not cause me to be overweight at the time, but I always suffered from fatigue, and it was difficult for me to stay awake in school. Every day I had to take a nap in order to function day-to-day. I am five feet nine inches, and my weight always stayed between 120 and 130 pounds. It stayed at 140 after I had my first child. I had a miscarriage when I was twenty-six, and my battle with weight problems started at that time. I rapidly gained weight, began to lose my hair, and started growing facial hair. It was not a happy time for me. I had always been thin, with a lush mane of dark hair and porcelain skin, so the new changes in my body were devastating. I went to Dr. Kwasman for the first time when I was twenty-six to try to lose weight, and I did lose weight, but I did not change my lifestyle. I didn't exercise or change the foods I was eating. I gained my weight back, and I used my health as an excuse of staying overweight. My health problems were part of the reason for my being overweight, but not exercising and eating the wrong foods contributed to the problem too. At age forty-eight, I decided I was no longer going to make excuses for my weight and decided to take responsibility and do something about it. I went to a doctor who told me my hormones were imbalanced and that is why I could not lose, so he put me on a hormone regimen to correct the imbalance. I lost thirty pounds after a few months, but then I stopped losing, and I still had over 100 pounds to lose. So I went back to Dr. Kwasman who provided nutritional counseling and worked with me on an individualized exercise program. Maybe you think you don't need to go to a doctor, but if you need to lose weight, being accountable to someone can help you. You might ask, "How do you know you won't gain the weight back?" The answer is a common theme you will see in this book: Choice, it's all about making good choices. I have chosen to change my way of living. I now choose to exercise daily, and I choose to eat the right foods. I can choose to go backwards, as people do for different reasons, but I choose to go forward in life healthy.

I realize there are health problems that people have that they can't control, but when you have health problems due to the choices you are making in life, you can make that step today and decide you want to live a better life. When people read the label on the cigarette package that smoking can cause cancer, heart problems, lung problems, and then go ahead and smoke, they are choosing to have bad health problems. If I choose to stop exercising or to go back to fried foods and a lot of starches, then I am choosing to gain weight. You have to make the choice to do whatever it takes to get healthy and commit to that choice. It might be difficult at first, but it will soon become part of your everyday life. I believe God wants us to be healthy. His Word tells us that, and as a Christian, I have been taught to stand on his Word and claim the promises of God. But the Bible also teaches that faith without works is dead. "Thus also faith by itself, if it does not have works, is dead" (James 2:17, NKJV). You have to make that difficult choice to take action to remain healthy. You have to make up your mind to change your bad habits that are causing you to continue in bad health.

Take Control of the Battle in your Mind

> You will keep him in perfect peace, whose mind is stayed on You, because he trusts in You. Trust in the Lord forever, for in YAH, the Lord, is everlasting strength.
>
> Isaiah 26:3–4 (NKJV)

Can you imagine being in perfect peace even during the difficult times that our world is facing right now? The economic issues appear to be getting worse instead of better. As pastors, we have to counsel even more people. There are people in more need now than we have seen since we began our ministry. If you can keep your mind on the Lord, you will be able to have peace during this time. This is a promise from God. When your mind is on the Lord, you are trusting in him, and he is your strength. When you are at peace, you can sleep at night. People consume energy drinks like water since they need the energy to get them through the day because of the lack of sleep the night before. They don't have strength because of restless nights. But when you are at peace with yourself, you can sleep at night. Many people have a battle going on in their mind and this keeps them up at night and robs them of the rest their body needs.

> For though we walk in the flesh, we do not war according to the flesh. For the weapons of our warfare are not carnal but mighty in God for pulling down strongholds, casting down arguments and every high thing that exalts itself against the knowledge of God, bringing every thought into captivity to the obedience of Christ.
>
> 2 Corinthians 10:3–5 (NKJV)

When something takes over your thought life, it is very hard to move forward. It can become a stronghold in your life if you don't get it under control. A stronghold starts with a single thought in the mind; that is why we are to take every thought captive. A stronghold will put you in bondage; most of the time the thought is a lie. The thought might be, *I can't live without that person.* The truth is you can. You might think, *I can't lose weight,* but the truth is you can. You could think, *I can't get a job; I'm not good enough.* The thought then can become a gripping fear, and fear will control you if you let it. Strongholds become idols because they are placed above God. The thoughts, the fears, and the strongholds begin to control you, and soon there is no place for God in your life. We are to bring down anything opposing God's will for our life, opposing the true knowledge of God the Father. What Paul is telling us in this scripture is to bring every disobedient thought into obedience to the Word of God.

Words that are spoken to us as children can become a stronghold in our mind if we choose to let them. That is why we must be careful with the words that come out of our mouth. Words can be used to bring healing or hurt. I remember an elderly woman who asked me for prayer. She said as a child her mother told her that she had wished she was never born, that she would amount to nothing, and was worthless. The lie that this mother told her child stayed with her even as an elderly woman. It became a stronghold in her life. She went through life never fulfilling the purpose for her life because she embraced her mother's lie. The lie tormented her mind. She never fit in anywhere because she thought she was worthless when the truth is, the Bible tells us:

> I will praise You, for I am fearfully and wonderfully made; Marvelous are Your works, and that my soul knows very well. My frame was not hidden from You, when I was made in secret, and skillfully wrought in the lowest parts of the earth. Your eyes saw my substance, being yet unformed, and in Your book they all were written, the days fashioned for me, when as yet there were none of them. How precious also are Your thoughts to me, O God! If I should count them, they would be more in number than the sand; When I awake, I am still with You.
>
> Psalm 139:14–18 (NKJV)

To think that the thoughts God has toward us are more than the number of sand. We were wonderfully and marvelously made by almighty God. Yet this woman believed the words that had been spoken to her as a young child instead of believing what the Word of God told her. When we allow tormenting thoughts to plague our mind, it is hard to function. My husband and I counsel with so many people who are tormented with what they assume people think of them. For example, sometimes thoughts enter their mind that their significant other is cheating on them, but there is no proof; it's just a thought that won't leave them. The lie that people believe as truth will destroy their relationship with other people. We are to cast down every vain imagination. People have accused others of things that never happened because of an imagination that was a lie. The imagination will have us believing problems are bigger than they really are. Vain imagination has caused people to think they are dying when they are in good health. Vain imagination can bring about mental illness. Assuming things that are false and allowing those thoughts to stay on our mind can soon become a stronghold. There are things that you have been told as a child but you know in your heart are a lie, so you need to choose to stop letting them torment you. Believe what the Word of God says about you. Choose to control your thoughts. Thoughts will come at you, but you can choose not to let them dwell there. When thoughts enter your mind that you know are lies, you have to make the choice to meditate on something else.

> But his delight is in the law of the Lord, and in His law he meditates day and night. He shall be like a tree planted by the rivers of water. That brings forth its fruit in its season, Whose leaf also shall not wither; And whatever he does shall prosper.
>
> Psalm 1:2–3 (NKJV)

A tree planted by a river becomes a strong tree. It is stable and it produces fruit; there is a purpose for the tree. It is being watered daily. When the winds come, it is not easily shaken or uprooted. It becomes strong because of the water it drinks. We need the Word of God to water us daily so we can be stable and we can be fruitful and productive. Paul said, "And do not be conformed to this world, but be transformed by the renewing of your mind, that you may prove what is that good and acceptable and perfect will of God" (Romans 12:2, NKJV). In other words, let the Word of God transform your life. Let truth control your way of thinking. Truth will cause you to change the things in your life that need changing. What we allow our mind to dwell on can cause us to be strong or weak. What we feed our mind and what we allow to stay there is very important. It's important not to allow negative things, false things, to control our way of thinking.

> Finally, brethren, whatever things are true, whatever things are noble, whatever things are just, whatever things are pure, whatever things are lovely, whatever things are of good report, if there is any virtue and if there is anything praiseworthy meditate on these things.
>
> Philippians 4:8 (NKJV)

Meditate on the good aspects of life; meditate on what you can do to make your life better. Choose to dwell on the good things that are happening in your life. Count your blessings instead of your troubles. We can choose what we think on. Random thoughts will intrude, but they don't have to stay. When we read about King Saul and King David, we see where Saul loved David as a son, but soon that love became tainted because he believed that the people loved David more. Jealousy consumed him. Saul began to resent David and wanted him dead. David loved Saul and stayed loyal to him, but because of the jealous thoughts that became strongholds in Saul's life, Saul wanted to kill David. Our thoughts can destroy everything around us when we allow them to control our life. You will find the story of Saul and David in 1 Samuel chapter 18. How sad it is when our thought patterns can cause relationships to break up. There might be times when God desires to place people in our life, but because of our thoughts, we don't let them get close to us. Saul began to think negative thoughts about David that soon turned to hatred, and then the thought of murder entered into his mind. He no longer could run his country because his mind was set on destroying David. He became crazy with these thoughts. He was no longer the leader he could have been. Iniquitous thinking can cause you to lose everything you worked so hard for in life. It will cause you to destroy your own dreams and then put the blame on someone else. It might be difficult to control your thought life, but if you work on it, you will soon be able to do it.

Words

Let the words of my mouth and the meditation of my heart be acceptable in Your sight, O Lord, my strength and my Redeemer.

Psalm 19:14 (NKJV)

Words are the most powerful tool we can use; they are a creative force. The words we speak can bring hope into someone's life, or they can destroy the last hope in an aching heart. Our words are powerful; they are spiritual seeds that we sow to bring forth a harvest. It is through words that we bring about a blessing or a cursing. Unfortunately, too many times, it's the latter rather than the former. "Death and life are in the power of the tongue: and they that love it shall eat the fruit thereof" (Proverbs 18:21, NKJV). The proverbs state that we will eat the fruit of our words. That is why we must be careful what fruit (words) we are sowing or planting.

God created the world with his words. He spoke; it happened. Genesis 1:3, "Then God said, 'Let there be light' and there was light." The Bible mentions many kinds of tongues (words):

- a flattering tongue (Psalm 5:9)
- a proud tongue (Psalm 12:3; 73:9)
- a lying tongue (Psalm 109:2; Proverbs 6:17)

- a deceitful tongue (Psalm 120:2)
- a perverted tongue (Proverbs 10:31; 17:20)
- a soothing tongue (Proverbs 15:4)
- a healing tongue (Proverbs 12:18)
- a destructive tongue (Proverbs 17:4)
- a mischievous and wicked tongue (Psalm 10:7)
- a soft tongue (Proverbs 25:15)
- a backbiting tongue (Proverbs 25:23)

We are often quick to say what comes into our mind, but we must always be mindful that we are responsible for the words that we speak. Jesus tells us,

> "But I say to you that for every idle word men may speak, they will give account of it in the day of judgment. For by your words you will be justified, and by your words you will be condemned"
> Matthew 12:36–37 (NKJV)

If we believed that we will be held accountable for every word we speak, we might be more careful how we use our words. We have a choice of how we use our words, and our words will help us to move forward or back and sometimes even destroy us. The book of Proverbs speaks of the virtuous wife and how she speaks, "She opens her mouth with wisdom, and on her tongue is the law of kindness" (Proverbs 31:26, NKJV). You can tell if someone is foolish or not when they open their mouth. There is a saying I often heard growing up: "It is better for someone to think you are a fool than for you to open your mouth and prove that you are one." Ecclesiastes speaks about words: "…and a fool's voice is known by his many words" (Ecclesiastes 5:3b, NKJV).

I recently taught a parenting class, and I was speaking to the mothers about the importance of how we speak to our children and admonished them to be careful what they call their children. So many times I have heard parents refer to their children in a negative way, calling them brats, rug rats, or other names. We can choose to sow negative seeds in our children's lives or sow positive seeds. When you encourage your child, your child will learn confidence. Children who are often put down by their parents grow up feeling condemned and not feeling good about themselves. "The wise woman builds her house, But the foolish pulls it down with her hands" (Proverbs 14:1, NKJV). I know this verse is speaking about how a wise woman through proper management increases the property and raiment of the household, and the thriftless woman causes these blessings to depart. But I have also seen women and men alike destroy their home by their words. They have dishonored one another by how they speak to each other. When you use your words to speak down to your spouse or your children, discourage them, or criticize them, you are pulling your house down. Anger will begin to build up in people who are always being condemned and yelled at. Your house is no longer a safe place for your family when you use your mouth against them. The wise person will build their house. When you build up people, you bless them with your mouth instead of cursing their path. Encourage people not by flattery but by using your words to speak life into people, allowing God to use you to speak his Word into people. Everything we do in the spirit realm is through our words. We worship with words, we pray with words, we cast out demons with words, and we speak blessings into lives with our words.

I went to Dr. Kwasman over twenty years ago, and his son at that time was four years old. He would speak about his son as though he was the greatest kid in the world, and through the years he would speak about how his son was going to go places in life; he was going to be a world changer. Dr. Kwasman was not just a father who was bragging about his son, but he was speaking blessings into his son's future. When my daughters were young, I had people tell me that when they grew up they were going to be a handful. I was always quick to rebuke their words and tell them that my daughters were going to be women of integrity, that they were my blessings from God and would continue being a blessing. I did not allow people to curse my daughters' pathway with their words. Now, I'm not speaking about superstition. I believe superstition is witchcraft; witchcraft is not of God, and God told us to have no part of it. I'm speaking what the Word of God says. His Word says, "Death and life are in the power of the tongue" (Proverbs 18:21, NKJV). So I encourage you today to pay close attention to how you use your words and see if your words are speaking life or death. Are you speaking negative things into your children's future? Are you tearing them down? Are you speaking negatively about your future? Are you telling people that you are never going to get a job, that you never get blessed? I believe what the Word of God says. Whatever comes out of your mouth, so be it. It becomes a self-fulfilling prophecy. That is what happens so many times, and people don't even realize what they are doing to themselves.

"There is one who speaks like the piercings of a sword, But the tongue of the wise promotes health" (Proverbs 12:18, NKJV). We can bring healing to people just by the words we speak. You can be used by God to bring healing to people's souls by your words. Isn't that awesome? We can begin to speak faith into our life situations. Learn and embrace the Word of God, so you can begin to stand on his Word and speak it. Choose to speak life to everything that you care about. When you allow this to become a part of your everyday life, you will begin to see your life transformed before your very eyes.

Living under an Open Heaven during an Economic Crisis

Blessed be the Lord, who daily loads us with benefits, the God of our salvation! Selah.

Psalm 68:19 (NKJV)

To live under an open heaven is to walk in the blessings of God no matter what is happening around you. You are being provided for; you are not worried about your housing, your food, and the clothes on your back because you're walking under an open heaven and trusting God for your provision. The Bible is very clear on how this can happen to you.

"Bring all the tithes into the storehouse, that there may be food in My house and try Me now in this," says the Lord of hosts, "If I will not open for you the windows of heaven and pour out for you such blessing that there will not be room enough to receive it. And I will rebuke the devourer for your sakes, so that he will not destroy the fruit of your ground, Nor shall the vine fail to bear fruit for you in the field," says the Lord of hosts.

Malachi 3:10–11 (NKJV)

I surely believe this is a fixed law that never changes. If we would just give God what belongs to him, he says he will open up the windows of heaven. He promises to give us a blessing that is measureless, blessings that are more than enough for you, blessings that will take care of your needs. God is actually inviting you to prove him in this by your giving. Reading in Malachi we also learn that we curse ourselves when we take what belongs to God.

> Will a man rob God? Yet you have robbed Me! But you say, 'In what way have we robbed You?' In tithes and offerings. You are cursed with a curse, for you have robbed Me, even this whole nation.
>
> Malachi 3:8–9 (NKJV)

I know that there are some who are reading this who don't believe in the Bible or in giving tithes and offerings. But I can say for myself that I have tried God in this and he has proven himself time and time again. In paying your tithes and offerings, you are telling God that you trust him. You are also acknowledging that everything you have belongs to him in the first place because he is the one who allowed you to have it. In 1 Kings 17, we read about the widow woman in Zarephath who gave the last of her food to Elijah.

> So he arose and went to Zarephath. And when he came to the gate of the city, indeed a widow was there gathering sticks. And he called to her and said, "Please bring me a little water in a cup, that I may drink." And as she was going to get it, he called to her and said, "Please bring me a morsel of bread in your hand." So she said, "As the Lord your God lives, I do not have bread, only a handful of flour in a bin,

and a little oil in a jar; and see, I am gathering a couple of sticks that I may go in and prepare it for myself and my son, that we may eat it, and die."

1 Kings 17:10–12 (NKJV)

We see where this woman had no hope. Her plans were to cook her last meal and then die with her son.

And Elijah said to her, "Do not fear; go and do as you have said, but make me a small cake from it first, and bring it to me; and afterward make some for yourself and your son. For thus says the Lord God of Israel: 'The bin of flour shall not be used up, nor shall the jar of oil run dry, until the day the Lord sends rain on the earth.'" So she went away and did according to the word of Elijah; and she and he and her household ate for many days. The bin of flour was not used up, nor did the jar of oil run dry, according to the Word of the Lord which He spoke by Elijah.

1 Kings 17:13–16 (NKJV)

Now you would think that God would have sent Elijah with food for the widow and her son, but instead her obedience to God is what helped her. She received an unfailing provision because of her trust in God. In giving, we don't give to help God out. He doesn't need your money. We give to help ourselves out; we give knowing that what we have belongs to God, and our giving is a form of worship to him. I have heard many people complain of the preachers who "take" money from the poor, the elderly, the widow, but what they don't realize is that these people know how to allow God to provide for them; they are giving a sacrifice offering to God, knowing that God will bless it. Being raised by a mother who was a widow, I had a chance to witness God's blessing time and time again, because my mother gave what she had to God, and God always provided for us.

I got my first job when I was sixteen, working at a cafeteria. I started saving my money to purchase a car. I would give most of my check to my mom, pay my tithes, and save the rest. After a while, I had $200 saved up. I was at church one Sunday when a visiting preacher was preaching. I don't remember the preacher or his sermon, but I felt in my spirit that God was telling me to give this man, whom I knew nothing about, the money that I had saved; the money I needed to purchase a car. I argued with God, I reminded God why I needed the money. *I need a car to go to church, work, and school.* This preacher already had a car, a nice one at that. If I gave the money, then I would have to start all over again to save what I lost, but if I kept it, then I would be disobeying what I knew God was telling me. I didn't understand why God would ask me to give what I worked so hard for. Most kids my age weren't even working. They just had to go to school and their parents purchased a car for them. I was working and going to school and going to church every time the doors were open. Didn't God know that? I did not want to give my money to some preacher I didn't know when I knew I needed the money more than he did. I kept hearing this small voice inside saying "Trust me, and give him the money as an offering to Me." Because I trusted in God, I obeyed what I knew in my heart God was telling me. I knew God wanted my obedience. He didn't need my money, but he wanted to see if I could trust him, and by obeying him I was showing him I trusted him. So I gave every penny of the $200 I had saved for my car to the preacher. I'm going to be honest. I did not do it with a merry heart.

A week later my pastor came to my house. I thought I was in trouble. He told my mom that he had just purchased a car for his wife, and he and his wife wanted to give me her car. He wanted to make sure it was okay with my mother. The car was only two years old with low mileage on it. On my own, I don't believe I could have ever saved for a car that new. My pastor had put new tires on it and had the oil changed. It looked like a brand new car. God opened the windows of heaven that day for me. I tried him and I continue trying him and God has never let me down.

We are to be a good steward in whatever God gives us. People have told me that they pay their tithes and offerings but they don't see the blessings of God. There are times when God will bless people and they waste what is given to them. People live beyond their means. People purchase things that they can't afford and don't need. When you charge something you cannot afford, and then you add that interest, you end up still paying for it months later; that is not being a good steward. That is wasting God's blessings. I know people who are behind in their bills, but when money comes in, they will blow it in one night at a restaurant and feel justified because they gave their tithes first. But their bills go unpaid because of the desire to reward themselves with food at a nice restaurant. We need to seek wisdom when it comes to money. People will purchase a luxury car when their budget is telling them they need a cheaper, more economical car, because they won't be able to afford the upkeep. Make a budget. If you can't pay your bills, then see what you are paying on and get rid of the excesses. Ask yourself the tough questions, like do you really need the super-deluxe cable package, Internet service, or cell phones for every member of the family? Look at ways to reduce or eliminate household expenses. What can you live without? Use wisdom in every purchasing decision.

Determine who in the household is wiser when it comes to paying bills and let that person handle the finances. If the bank tells you that you can have that loan, but you know in your heart you cannot afford to repay it, just say, "No, thank you." We live in a world of excess and don't really need all the "stuff" we tend to accumulate. Get rid of the excess items you have. Sell them for extra cash, or better yet, donate them to needy families who really do need them. Begin to put money in savings, even if it's just a nominal amount. You will be surprised at how quickly it adds up! Get rid of your expensive habits. If you are a good steward over everything that is given to you, then you will find that you can live on less if you need to. If your household is running on one income, then live within the means of one income. Our parents did it. They bought a house when they could afford it and they bought furniture when the money was available. Instead of having a "I need it right now" mindset, we need to go back to "We will get it when we can afford it, we can wait" mindset. Be thankful for what you do have. Don't complain about what you don't have or need, because there is always someone with less than you. It's like the man who thanked God for his feet even though he had no shoes because he knew that there were people without feet. You see, God has blessed many people, but many people choose not to be good stewards about what is given them. When the "windows of heaven" open up on you, you must use wisdom.

I had a mother come to me telling me how poor she was, she was crying, saying she did not understand why God wouldn't bless her. Her children wore expensive brand-name clothing and shoes. She had fine, beautiful jewelry, but she could not pay her bills. Granted, she was not wealthy; she was a single mother of several children, but she bought whatever the children wanted. She lived like she was wealthy. She wanted her children to have what other children had. Instead of teaching her children values, she taught them that material things were important. Material things are nice to have, but when they control your life, you will never have enough money to keep up that momentum. If you don't know how to be a good steward over small things, you will not be able to be a good steward over large things. Begin to keep your spending habits in check. Take care of the debts you have now before you make any more debt. Keep a record of all your expenses. Live frugally and take notice of your utility consumption. For example, turn off lights when possible; use your dryer in the early morning or evening. Open the windows instead of switching on the air conditioning. Take care of your health. Make sure you are keeping your car in good shape so you don't have to get another one or face expensive automotive repair bills.

When you begin to be a good steward over everything God has given you, you will begin to see the blessings in your life. I truly believe if we allow God to direct us, he will show us how to save money and make money. Begin to use the talents God has given you. If you are artistic, make things and sell them. Ask friends for contacts, such as your hairdresser, and see if you can leave things in the shop to be sold. If you sing, begin calling wedding planners and funeral directors and let them know you are willing to sing for a small fee. Use what God has given you, and watch the talents that you were born with become blessings in your life financially. You see, sometimes the blessings are right there in us, but we are doing nothing with them. If we don't use the gifts that are within us, how can we expect more from God when we are doing nothing with the gifts we have? "And all these blessings shall come upon you and overtake you, because you obey the voice of the Lord your God" (Deuteronomy 28:2, NKJV).

I Hear the Sound of an Abundance of Rain

You, O God, sent a plentiful rain, Whereby You
confirmed Your inheritance, when it was weary. Your
congregation dwelt in it; You, O God, provided from
Your goodness for the poor.

Psalm 68:9 (NKJV)

During a time of drought, we pray for rain. America is in
a drought and we need an outpouring of rain. God is the
rainmaker! We read in 1 Kings chapter 18 that there was a
drought in the land for three years due to Ahab's failure to
acknowledge the Lord, Ahab and Israel worshiped Baal
instead. In chapter 18 we read there was a contest, or a
showdown, between the Hebrew God and Baal. I remember hearing this story as a young child and I loved it. God
has proven himself time and time again, and in this story
he did so again.

So Ahab sent for all the children of Israel, and
gathered the prophets together on Mount Carmel.
And Elijah came to all the people, and said, "How
long will you falter between two opinions? If the
Lord is God, follow Him; but if Baal, follow him."
But the people answered him not a word. Then
Elijah said to the people, "I alone am left a prophet

of the Lord; but Baal's prophets are four hundred and fifty men."

1 Kings 18:20–22 (NKJV)

Elijah was telling the people, "You need to make up your mind who you are going to serve." Many times we want to go with the crowd, whatever the majority thinks, whoever is the most popular, and we forget the teachings of our youth. We forget what God has already done for us and the drought comes because of it. Because of our choices, the drought hits us, not because of God, but because of what or who we decide to serve. Now the contest was to take place on Mount Carmel. The Canaanites built sanctuaries to pagan weather deities on this mountain. What a perfect place for God to show himself! All of Israel was there to observe. The contest was for the prophets of Baal to prepare a bull and put it on wood with no fire under it, and Elijah was going to do the same with another bull. The prophets of Baal were to cry out to their gods and Elijah would cry out to the Lord and whoever answered by fire would be God. The prophets of Baal spent six hours crying out to their god with no response; they even cut themselves with knives and lances to plea to their god and nothing happened, but then came Elijah's turn to cry out to his Lord. Before he prayed, he had water poured on the altar he had made in the name of the Lord, and water filled a trench around the altar. Water had soaked the wood.

> And it came to pass, at the time of the offering of the evening sacrifice, that Elijah the prophet came near and said, "Lord God of Abraham, Isaac, and Israel, let it be known this day that You are God in

Israel and I am Your servant, and that I have done all these things at Your Word. Hear me, O Lord! Hear me, that this people may know that You are the Lord God, and that You have turned their hearts back to You again." Then the fire of the Lord fell and consumed the burnt sacrifice, and the wood and the stones and the dust, and it licked up the water that was in the trench. Now when all the people saw it, they fell on their faces; and they said, "The Lord, He is God! The Lord! He is God!"

1 Kings 18:26–39 (NKJV)

Elijah stood against four hundred and fifty prophets of Baal. He did not back down; he knew whom he was serving. During the hard times, you need to know who you are serving and praying to. Elijah said to Ahab, "Go up, eat and drink; for there is the sound of abundance of rain" (1 Kings 18:41, NKJV). The drought ended; Elijah heard the sound of an abundance of rain when there were no clouds to be seen. He prayed seven times, and the seventh time his servant told him there was a cloud, as small as a man's hand, rising out of the sea and then a heavy rain came. Now the six different times that Elijah sent his servant out there was no sign whatsoever of rain. It didn't smell like rain, it didn't look like rain, but Elijah heard the rumblings of what God was about to do. Elijah heard a miracle getting ready to happen; he heard the sound of restoration. He heard the sound of abundance, not just a small thing that was getting ready to happen, but an abundance of things getting ready to happen.

There are times that we pray and do everything according to the Word of God and we get nothing. During this time when we feel that nothing is happening, our prayers are hitting the walls, and we feel that we are not reaching heaven, is the time to keep your ear attuned to God. Don't give up! That is when you have to have faith and stand on the Word of God, knowing that he hears you even when you see nothing happening. Stay in prayer. Elijah stayed in prayer, and on the seventh time, his servant came back saying that he saw a cloud shaped like a man's hand, rising out of the sea; the cloud wasn't even in the sky. Elijah knew that this was the hand of the Lord God and God was getting ready to make it rain. When we serve the Lord, we have a promise from him of his provision. The coming of the rain was the final proof that the Lord God of Israel was supreme. God wants us to have plenty of rain in our lives. God has more than enough to provide for you. He wants to rain his Spirit, blessings, provision, peace, and joy on you and your loved ones.

Rain brings refreshment and cleansing. We need the rain for growth. It clears the air. When things begin to look impossible in your life, that is the time to praise God, pray to him, and expect him to take care of you. His provision may come in ways you never thought of, from sources you know nothing about, but choose to trust him, no matter how overwhelming the drought is in your life. If you choose to serve the gods of Baal, then you will have to choose to reap the consequences of those choices. God created us all, but only those who choose him as their God reap the benefits of the promises that he gives. I desire to dwell in his abundance of rain, and I know if I trust him to be my source, I will. When we do all we know to do according to his Word, we can trust God to do the rest.

Making Time for God in Our Hurried Life

> And she said to her husband, 'Look now, I know that this is a holy man of God, who passes by us regularly. Please, let us make a small upper room on the wall; and let us put a bed for him there, and a table and a chair and a lampstand; so it will be, whenever he comes to us, he can turn in there.'
>
> 2 Kings 4:9–10 (NKJV)

Elisha, the prophet of God, often traveled through Shunem, stopping at the Shunammite woman's home where he would be fed. She recognized that God was with him. I believe she could feel God's anointing in her home when Elisha came by. She wanted the presence of God to be in her home. By making room for the man of God, she was making room for God to dwell there also. Instead of wanting God to center his life on her, she centered her life on God. So many times we make a plan for our life and ask God to bless it, instead of seeking God for his plan for our life and embracing it. She saw an opportunity to do something for God, and she took advantage of the opportunity. When you see an open door to be a blessing, walk in the door; act upon it.

When I was a child, we would often go to my grandparents' house where they had "family prayer time" three times a day. Morning, noon, and night, we stopped whatever we were doing to get together to pray, read Scriptures, and sing worship to God for an hour. I did not appreciate the value of this exercise at the time. As a child, I saw more value in playtime, and I wanted to keep playing outside with my brother. Now I look back and I appreciate the strong upbringing I had in God. It taught me that he should come first in everything we do, that God should be the center of my life, and I was to put him first. My grandparents did not expect God to work on their schedule. They made sure that he was the main focus of their day. You see, they truly valued their relationship with God.

There are people who call me and want me to pray on their behalf because they believe I have a straight line to heaven. Frankly, I believe I do too, not because I'm special or because God loves me more, but because I have made him a very important part of my life. My relationship with God is valuable to me. When you have a relationship with someone you care about, you work on developing the relationship. You find out what that person likes and you look for mutual areas of interest. You make it your goal to find out what is important to them and what makes them happy. You do things to make the relationship stronger. We are willing to sacrifice our wants at times in order to develop a relationship with someone we have strong feelings for. We want to spend a lot of time with that person.

Developing a relationship with God is the same way. I was blessed to start my relationship with God as a small child, and the more I communicated with him the more I was able to recognize when he was speaking to me. God will speak to us in many ways, but until and unless we start talking to him, we won't learn how he speaks to us. God speaks to me through dreams, and sometimes in a small, still voice within. Sometimes it is through other people, and always we can hear from him by reading his Word. We have to read his Word to get to know more about him. The more we communicate with him the more we will get to know his voice. I know without a doubt that God hears my prayers. I communicate with him daily. Many times God awakens me at three a.m. Heaven is on a different timetable than Arizona, I suppose, but maybe that is a time that God knows he will have my undivided attention without the distraction of phones or interruption of people. So when God desires time with me and nudges me from my sleep, I make time because I love talking with him. It is a love relationship, a perfect Father/daughter relationship. He desires time with you, too, when nothing and no one will get in the way and it is just you and him. Sometimes it might be a sacrifice of your time, but when you start giving time to God, you will soon desire and seek that time with him yourself. I really don't consider myself a religious person, but I do know I have a one-on-one relationship with God. He has never failed me. There are times that he tells me "no." Many times, in fact, but I know that there is nothing too trivial to bring to him.

Have you ever been in someone's home and you could not wait to leave because there was so much unrest in the home, no peace? You might even say it wasn't a home but just a house with people in it. The home did not have the peace of God resting in it. Then there are homes you go into and you feel peace. You might be having a bad day, but as soon as you walked in the home you felt the heaviness leave you and a peace envelope you. The very presence of God was in the home. The people who live there were filled with the peace of God, and their home was too.

When you allow the presence of God in your life, you will soon receive his presents, which are many. If you continue reading the story of the Shunammite woman, you will see that God blessed her and her husband with a son, even though her husband was already an old man. Her son later died of heat stroke, but God raised the young boy up and restored him. In chapter 8, of 2 Kings, Elisha warned the Shunammite woman first of the famine that was going to come for seven years. Then he told her to leave her home and she listened to the man of God. When she returned after seven years she saw someone was living in her home, but God gave her favor with the king. The king gave her house and all the proceeds of the field for the seven years she was gone, back to her. God's blessings were upon this woman because she made room for him. Because of this, she was warned of trouble and told what to do to protect herself and her family. Because she was open to communication, she heard God.

There are times that we want blessings from God, but we don't want to make any time for him. We cry out to him when everything is going wrong, but we ignore God when everything is going right. In order to walk in the blessings of God, we have to make room for him to enter. You cannot expect to get a paycheck at work if you have not given any time to your job; you know that you have to show up to work. God is ready to show up in our life when we allow him to. When we make room, when we give him our time instead of expecting him to just give his time, he will be there for us in our lives, but remember that God will not force himself on us. God is not an errand boy that we can just call on to do things for us whenever we have a need. He is, however, a loving Father ready to bless us and guide us if we just call on his name.

The Shunammite woman saw a need and did something about it. She made room for the man of God without even thinking of what she would get in return. When we begin to do for others just because we want to or because we see a need, we will reap blessings in return. When we wake up thinking, *What can I do to help someone today?* we will forget about the problems and worries in our life and soon we will be living in the blessing of God. Soon your home will be a home where people walk in and feel the presence of God.

We have all heard the saying, "It is better to give then to receive." That is what the Shunammite woman did, and God blessed her with a son. Even though her husband was an old man, he was able to plant the seed to produce that son. God is in the blessing business when we make the room for the blessings. In fact, he wants to bless us! The Shunammite woman was a very busy woman; she and her husband had a big farm to care for. Farmers and their wives worked from sun up to sun down, and the Shunammite woman still made room and time in her busy life for God.

When Everything Is Wrong, Trust God to Make Things Right

In You, O Lord, I put my trust; Let me never be ashamed; Deliver me in Your righteousness.

Psalm 31:1 (NKJV)

Trusting God when everything is going wrong seems an impossible task. Recognizing and acknowledging that is a very difficult thing to do, but know always that it can be done. Job was truly a man who trusted God when everything was going wrong in his life. Job not only had faith in God but also trusted him. I've seen people keep tremendous faith until things started going wrong in their life and then their faith in God diminished.

In the story of Job, God gave Satan permission to try Job's faith. Job lost his wealth, his children, and his health. Yet Job still trusted God and held fast to his integrity. He did not know why all these things had fallen upon him, but he still trusted God and remained steadfast in his beliefs. After finding out that he lost all his children and all his wealth, this is what Job did:

> Then Job arose, tore his robe, and shaved his head; and he fell to the ground and worshiped. And he said: "Naked I came from my mother's womb, And naked shall I return there. The Lord gave, and the

Lord has taken away; Blessed be the name of the Lord." In all this Job did not sin nor charge God with wrong.

Job 1:20–22 (NKJV)

By giving worship to God after he had lost everything, Job did the complete opposite of what most people would do. Job did not just talk faith, he walked his faith. Worshiping God in the midst of your storm is telling God, "You're still my God no matter what comes against me." Worship is a selfless act that we give. God loves to hear worship. I heard a news reporter speak about Pastor Benny Hinn once, and they shared how he used worship to hype people up. I knew when I heard the news reporter that he must not know or even begin to understand what worship does for God. Worship will bring an atmosphere of peace in your home. When you begin to worship God, it can bring healing to your innermost being. Worship to God moves his very heart. I have seen many miracles happen during a worship service. I don't know much about Pastor Benny Hinn, but one thing I do know is he has worship music to hype God up, not the people. Worship will bring the right kind of atmosphere for the miracles of God to happen. Worship to God can cause depression and oppression to leave. When you worship God, you can expect change to happen. The best thing you can do when you are going through a life storm is worship God. Change the atmosphere in your home by putting worship music on and start praising God while in your storm.

We see where Job never blamed God; he acknowledged that it was God who gave to him. If God chose to take it away then God has the right to take it back. Job recognized that all he had belonged to God in the first place. Job had many possessions, but he did not allow those possessions to have him. Job put God first in his life. His possessions did not come before God, nor did his family.

I cannot imagine going through the hurt and pain that Job went through and then watch his friends judge and condemn him. Job's friends judged him and told him that he needed to repent because they believed he had sinned, causing these things to happen to him. Even today some preachers say Job suffered these trials because of his fear. But it is important to note that the Bible said Job was blameless, upright, and one who feared God. God knew that he could trust Job to trust him no matter what storm he had to go through. It is one thing to trust God, but can God trust you? Can he trust you to serve him when life is unfair to you? Can God trust you to still love him when everything comes crashing down on you? Your relationship with God is taken to a whole other level when God can trust you. That is the relationship I want to have with God the almighty.

Job says, "Though He slay me, yet will I trust Him" (Job 13:15, NKJV). Oh, what faith Job had! I believe Job was able to trust God because Job had such a loving and trusting relationship with him. It would be impossible to totally trust God if you have not formed a close relationship with him.

Some might be concerned that Job questioned God. Know that it is okay to question God. In having a close relationship with God, I question him all the time, and yes, I will even admit that I have gotten angry sometimes with the decisions he has made. But in the end, I know in my heart that our Father, in his omnipotence, always knows what's best for me. Like any good parent/ child relationship, he makes the decisions that he knows will benefit me both spiritually and personally. God knew Job, and he knew what Job was able to handle. Job did not know why God was allowing these things to happen to him, and yet he trusted God. Let us learn from Job's story. We should not be like Job's friends. We should never assume that because someone is going through a trial or sickness that it is because of their sin. We should always be ready to encourage, comfort, and strengthen those who are going through a difficult time. When someone is going through a trial, that is not the time to get sanctimonious toward them. Even as a pastor, when people start acting self-righteous, I want to run the other way. Religious people are quick to talk the talk, but can you worship God and stay true to your faith when everything is coming against you?

The Battle Is Not Yours

> And he said, 'Listen, all you of Judah and you inhabitants of Jerusalem, and you, King Jehoshaphat! Thus says the Lord to you: Do not be afraid nor dismayed because of this great multitude, for the battle is not yours, but God's.'
>
> 2 Chronicles 20:15 (NKJV)

This is one of my favorite stories in the Hebrew Scriptures. However, they are not just stories but an account of things that really happened. The Scripture gives us hope and guidance even hundreds of years later. What God did for Jehoshaphat he can do for us. Let us refer to 2 Chronicles chapter 20. It tells us that Jehoshaphat was the king of Judah and a great multitude was coming against him. In verse 3 it tells us that Jehoshaphat was afraid, and he sought the Lord and proclaimed a fast throughout all Judah. When you are afraid of your circumstances, the first thing you need to do is:

1) Seek God and fast:

So many times we seek friends and family for their advice. We will even seek ungodly advice before we seek God's face. If you are going through a difficult time in your life and things are looking hopeless, impossible even to deal with, seek God before you do anything else. Get on your knees and cry out to him. Fast and pray, and if you can't fast from food because of health problems, fast from TV or something else that takes your time. Use that time to pray and seek him. God tells us in his Word how to call on him and get God to give us his ear so he will hear us:

If My people who are called by My name will humble themselves, and pray and seek My face, and turn from their wicked ways, then I will hear from heaven, and will forgive their sin and heal their land.
2 Chronicles 7:14 (NKJV)

Then we read where Jehoshaphat acknowledges who God is:

O Lord God of our fathers, are You not God in heaven, and do You not rule over all the kingdoms of the nations, and in Your hand is there not power and might, so that no one is able to withstand You?
2 Chronicles 20:6 (NKJV)

2) Acknowledge who God is:

When we acknowledge who God is and how powerless we are, we are humbling ourselves. We are living in a day where everyone is saying we need to build our self-esteem, when the truth is we need to deflate our self-esteem and real-ize that without God, we are nothing. God is the one who is all powerful. I have heard people boast about the company they have pioneered by themselves, how they are a hard worker, or how they put themselves through school. And while that might be true, they need to recognize that without God they would not have been able to do any of those things. You see, it is God who grants us the mercy to wake up with a sound mind. It is God who, through his mercy, who gives us another day. So it is God that we need to give thanks to for giving us another day to accomplish what needs to be done.

Jehoshaphat begins to tell God what God had done before for his people.

> Are You not our God, who drove out the inhabitants of this land before Your people Israel, and gave it to the descendants of Abraham Your friend forever? And they dwell in it, and have built You a sanctuary in it for Your name, saying, "If disaster comes upon us—sword, judgment, pestilence, or famine—we will stand before this temple and in Your presence (for Your name is in this temple), and cry out to You in our affliction, and You will hear and save."
>
> 2 Chronicles 20:7–9 (NKJV)

3) Remind God of what his Word says and what he did for his people:

Before Jehoshaphat reminded God of what he did for Abraham and the promise that he gave Abraham, he told God, "You said, You will hear us and save us, God" (2 Chronicles 20:9).

Whenever I have made promises to my children, they are always quick to remind me of the promise, and that is what Jehoshaphat did to God. You need to know what the Word of God says in order to remind him. Know God's Word for yourself, that way you don't have to depend on other people to tell you what the Word says. Find out what the promises of God are. I sing a song titled "He'll Do It Again," and the chorus goes,

"He is still God, and he will not fail you, I know that he is God, and he's fighting for you, just like Moses, just like Daniel, just like Shadrach, Meshach, and Abednego. He'll do it again."

Just like he was there for the three Hebrew boys and for Moses and Daniel, he will be there for you. "For I am the Lord, I do not change" (Malachi 3:6a, NKJV).

As we read further on, Jehoshaphat acknowledges that he and his army have no power.

"O our God, will You not judge them? For we have no power against this great multitude that is coming against us; nor do we know what to do, but our eyes are upon You."

2 Chronicles 20:12 (NKJV)

4)   Keep your eyes upon God:

Don't get distracted by what other people are doing. Be obedient to the Word of God and you cannot go wrong. When we are going through a storm in our life, it is so easy to take our eyes off God and focus on the storm. We keep our eyes on the problem instead of focusing on the solution, when, in fact, the solution is God. If we can keep our eyes on God, then we won't have to deal with worry. Worry comes when we focus on the problem. There are times when worry will make the problem appear bigger than it really is. Worry will also cause you to see how impossible the problem is, and then it is harder to trust God to provide a solution.

In verse 14 we read how the Spirit of God came upon Jahaziel and gave him a message to give to King Jehoshaphat and to the people of Judah and Jerusalem:

And he said, 'Listen, all you of Judah and you inhabitants of Jerusalem, and you, King Jehoshaphat! Thus says the Lord to you: 'Do not be afraid nor dismayed because of this great multitude, for the battle is not yours, but God's.'

2 Chronicles 20:15 (NKJV)

5) Listen when God speaks; give him control; give him the battle:

Listen to the people of God. When I was getting ready to marry for the first time, my pastor, who was a true man of God, told me it was not God's will for me to marry the person I was engaged to. Pastor Bob Laughlin knew God had called me into the ministry, and he told me that even though this young man was in the church now, within two years he would leave the church and we would not go into ministry. He also told me I would be unhappy and unfulfilled because I would not be in the will of God. I knew that my pastor had heard that message from God, and I felt an uncertainty in my spirit, but I was young and starry-eyed and in love, and I did not listen to the message that God had given my pastor. I married, and in two years, just as prophesied, my husband left not only the church but also God. He said he wanted no part of God. He started living a lifestyle that I could not embrace or condone. After twelve years of marriage, he left me and told me as long as I was living for God and he was running from God, he could not be with me. We had two beautiful children, and I thank God for them, but they were hurt just as much as I was by the end of our marriage. People asked me if I questioned God and asked why he let this happen to me. I had to say, "No." I went through heartache and pain because I chose not to listen to the man of God. Now I know not every preacher hears from God. A lot of people will say, "God said," and they are instead sharing what they personally feel. When God speaks through someone, you will know it is God because it will bear witness with what you already are feeling. It will line up with his Word. If it goes against the Bible, then you know it is not God. God usually will speak to your heart first and then has someone tell you in order to confirm it.

Going through the divorce was difficult, but it gave me an opportunity to give my battle to God. I became a single mother of a two-year-old and a nine-year-old. God brought me and my girls through the hardships of divorce and single parenthood, but I believe that only happened because I gave it over to God.

You will not need to fight in this battle. Position yourselves, stand still, and see the salvation of the Lord, who is with you, O Judah and Jerusalem! Do not fear or be dismayed; tomorrow go out against them, for the Lord is with you.

2 Chronicles 20:17 (NKJV)

6)   Position yourselves, stand still, and see God fight for you; face your fears:

In the midst of a raging storm, it goes against our every instinct to stand still, but that is what God told the king to do: position yourself, stand still, and watch me fight for you. God also told them to go out against them. In other words, they positioned themselves right where the battle was to be. They had to face the enemy. I believe if I were King Jehoshaphat, I would have wanted to flee, running as fast as possible in the opposite direction! A great multitude was coming to kill him and all his people. But God's instruction was simply to stand still. Don't do anything. How difficult that must have been for King Jehoshaphat! When we are facing a great storm in our life, we want to do something.

It is difficult to be still and wait. We have all heard someone say, "I just can't stand here and do nothing." God did not tell Jehoshaphat to prepare his men to fight, nor did he tell him to flee or bar the doors. He simply said to get in position and stand still. When we allow God to fight for us, we will see the reward after the storm. If we say, "No God, I can handle this myself, I don't need your help," then the storm will get bigger and impossible to control. Get in line with God's Word. Be in position and attuned to hear from God. If you have stopped talking to him, you are not in position, you are not standing still. If you are negative or surround yourself with negative people, you are not in position, you are not standing still. If you are on the side of the enemy, then you're not in position, and you are certainly not standing still for God. How can you be on the side of the enemy? By not complying with the Bible; by doing things your way.

Position yourself to see what God is doing for you. Stand still. "Be still, and know that I am God; I will be exalted among the nations, I will be exalted in the earth!" (Psalm 46:10, NKJV). Be still and begin to know who God is. Ask the Lord to make your mind still so you can have peace. There are times when we are so focused on the negative things that we can't even see God working for us. Look for the blessings because they abound. "And Jehoshaphat bowed his head with his face to the ground, and all Judah and the inhabitants of Jerusalem bowed before the Lord, worshiping the Lord" (2 Chronicles 20:18, NKJV).

7) Don't forget to give God the glory and worship him:

> So they rose early in the morning and went out into the Wilderness of Tekoa; and as they went out, Jehoshaphat stood and said, "Hear me, O Judah and you inhabitants of Jerusalem: Believe in the Lord your God, and you shall be established; believe his prophets, and you shall prosper." And when he had consulted with the people, he appointed those who should sing to the Lord, and who should praise the beauty of holiness, as they went out before the army and were saying; "Praise the Lord, For His mercy endures forever."
>
> 2 Chronicles 20:20–21 (NKJV)

The chapter ends with the battle being won by the Lord. King Jehoshaphat and his army just praised God, and God did the work. The enemy killed one another. King Jehoshaphat did not have to do any fighting. They just had to position themselves, stand still, and watch God move. I believe that was the most difficult thing for King Jehoshaphat to do, but he did it, and God kept his promise. At the end of the day, they got such an abundance of valuables that it took three days to gather it. When the men of Judah and Jerusalem returned with Jehoshaphat, they remembered to give God praise and the glory, and they rejoiced in what God had done for them. What a valuable spiritual lesson you and I can take away from this!

There's a Battle in the Spiritual Realm

> I will love You, O Lord, my strength. The Lord is my rock and my fortress and my deliverer, My God, my strength, in whom I will trust; My shield and the horn of my salvation, my stronghold.
>
> Psalm 18:1–2 (NKJV)

2 Kings chapter 6 tells the story about Elisha, the prophet. God was using him to warn the King of Israel how the king of Syria, Ben-Hadad, was making war against them and what the enemy had planned. God told Elisha every time Ben-Hadad was going to attack and where, and King Ben-Hadad thought that one of his own men was a spy for Israel. Then one of his servants told him, "It is Elisha, the prophet who is in Israel, tells the king of Israel the words that you speak in your bedroom" (2 Kings 6:12, NKJV). So when King Ben-Hadad heard this, he decided he was going to have Elisha killed.

> Therefore he sent horses and chariots and a great army there, and they came by night and surrounded the city. And when the servant of the man of God arose early and went out, there was an army, surrounding the city with horses and chariots. And his servant said to him, "Alas, my master! What shall we do?" So he answered, "Do not fear, for those who

are with us are more than those who are with them."
And Elisha prayed, and said, "Lord, I pray open his
eyes that he may see." Then the Lord opened the
eyes of the young man, and he saw. And behold, the
mountain was full of horses and chariots of fire all
around Elisha.

2 Kings 6:14–17 (NKJV)

When Elisha told his servant, "Those who are with us
are more than those who are with them," I'm sure his servant became even more fearful. It is bad enough having
an army surrounding you with vengeance in their hearts
and plans to kill you, but Elisha saw things. The servant
counted only himself and Elisha, but Elisha saw more
than the army surrounding him. Elisha was able to look
past his circumstances and see into the spiritual realm.
And in the spiritual realm he saw where God had him
more than covered. God was on his job, taking care of
Elisha and his servant.

I believe Elisha had a personal relationship with God,
which was more than just a religious bond. There are
many religious people in the world who have no real relationship with God. Elisha, I believe, had a special one-on-
one, deeply personal relationship with God, and he loved
and trusted him. He had faith that God was going to take
care of this matter. When you fall in love with God, you
will begin to trust him with your life. That is where Elisha
was in his relationship with God. Elisha saw what the
mortal eye could not see. He saw God's army surrounding
him, so he knew there was no need to worry. Elisha then
asked God to also reveal this to his servant, and God did
just that. When we feel surrounded by difficulty in our
life and we feel that escape is impossible, we must ask and

believe God will help us see through our spiritual vision rather than our natural vision. When you feel there is no hope for your situation, or your children are headed down a rocky path and you feel there is no hope for them, ask God to let you see their life through his eyes. Know that when we are serving God while we are on God's side, he is also on our side! There is always hope, always.

> For I know the thoughts that I think toward you," says the Lord, "thoughts of peace and not of evil, to give you a future and a hope. Then you will call upon Me and go and pray to Me, and I will listen to you, And you will seek me and find Me, when you search for Me with all your heart.
>
> Jeremiah 29:11–13 (NKJV)

Another translations reads: "For I know the plans I have for you," says the Lord. "They are plans for good and not for disaster, to give you a future and a hope" (Jeremiah 29:11–13, NIV). Know this: God has you in his thoughts, he has your loved ones in his thoughts. We just have to turn to him, go to him, and seek him out. This is a scripture I have stood on from a child. When I have gone through the many life storms, one thing that has helped sustain me has been to say, "God I know you have a plan for my life. Your thoughts are toward me. You have given me a future and a hope, and I am standing and believing on your Word, for you are a God who does not lie." Seek him out and know that God is ready to hear your cry. This one thing I know: I would not have been born if God did not have a plan for me.

There is a purpose and a future for your life, but unless you seek God for yourself, you will not know that purpose. The reason some people are depressed and unhappy in their life is because they are not walking in their purpose. When you are not walking the path that God has for you, your life will be unfulfilled.

Walking in Holiness

Speak to all the congregation of the sons of Israel and say to them, 'You shall be holy, for I the Lord your God am holy.'

> Leviticus 19:2 (NKJV)

For I am the Lord who brings you up out of the land of Egypt, to be your God. You shall therefore be holy, for I am holy.

> Leviticus 11:45 (NKJV)

How on earth can we be holy like God? Why would God tell us to be holy if it is an impossible thing? Through the years, man has had his own interpretation on what is holy and what is not. God gave laws to the Hebrew people to follow in order to be holy. God gave us his Word to show us.

Growing up, I was taught by different people that a woman was holy if she didn't cut her hair and wore long dresses with long sleeves (those women probably did not have to endure the heat of the Arizona desert). We were taught you were holy if you didn't go to movies or swim. Almost everything was a sin except going to church. If you went to church every Sunday morning, Sunday night, and Wednesday night, and Friday night prayer, then you were surely holy. Then I grew up and realized that holiness had to come from the inside and work itself out.

So what is holiness? One thing we can do is look at God's character, because God is holy and he tells us to be like him. We see that God is a loving God who shows mercy, and he is very good at forgiving. The closer we walk with God, the more we will take on his character. God tells us in the following scripture to be holy; it's not a suggestion, but a command: "You shall be holy." I don't believe God would tell us to do something that is impossible for us to do. Walking in holiness is walking in forgiveness, granting mercy to people who sometimes don't deserve mercy, and walking in love. Being holy is taking on the character of God. It is a choice. We choose whether we want to be more like our heavenly Father, or we choose to rebel against his Word, just as our children choose to listen to our instructions or choose to rebel against them.

My husband and I have a blended family. I had two daughters, and my husband had two sons and a daughter when we married. We let our children know as Joshua did that our house was going to be a home where God dwells.

> And if it seems evil unto you to serve the Lord, choose you this day whom ye will serve; whether the gods which your fathers served that were on the other side of the flood, or the gods of the Amorites, in whose land ye dwell; but as for me and my house, we will serve the Lord.
>
> Joshua 24:15 (NKJV)

We chose to raise our children up in the way of the Lord, teaching them to walk in love, forgiveness, showing mercy, and following God's Word. Joshua made a strong statement to the people of Israel: you have a choice to serve the gods of the world or the one true God. And he decided it was the Hebrew God that he and his household were going to serve. When we make that choice and we serve the Lord and seek his face, he will be faithful to show us the plan he has for us and help us to walk in holiness, and that path will bring fulfillment in our lives.

Walking in holiness will separate you from the rest of the world. Your choices will be different, and people won't always understand why you do the things you do. When I was going through a divorce from my first husband, my pastor told me that I should do nothing but show love and stay in an attitude of forgiveness. Now, that was easy for him to say; he had never been through a divorce. I thought to myself, *What kind of advice is that?* Another minister told me I should take him to court and get everything I could and get him before he gets me. At the time, that is the kind of advice my broken heart wanted to hear, especially since there was another woman involved. I confess that I temporarily forgot to walk in holiness because all I could think about at that moment was how much I wanted to snatch her bald headed and beat her up! After all, I reasoned to myself, I had a right to be angry and was justified in expressing that anger. I was raised with five brothers, and I knew how to fight. I had two young children, ages nine and two. They were hurting, and that made me all the angrier. In the end, reason prevailed, and I soon had to remind myself about walking in holiness always, not just when it's convenient or easy.

People often say that the hard thing is usually the right thing to do. Daily walking in love, mercy, and forgiveness is difficult, but it will keep you walking in freedom. It will keep your mind free. I knew my pastor was telling me the truth. It would have been easier to get a lawyer and make things ugly for my soon-to-be ex-husband, and I would had felt justified, but I chose to follow my pastor's advice, and in the long run, it made it easier for me to heal from the pain of the separation and divorce.

> For if you forgive men their trespasses, your heavenly Father will also forgive you. But if you do not forgive men their trespasses, neither will your Father forgive your trespasses.
>
> Matthew 6:14 (NKJV)

When you walk around angry, unwilling to forgive, and carrying reproach in your heart, it will weigh you down. It turns into bitterness and festers, hardening your heart, narrowing your vision, and staying with you for years. The person who you decide not to forgive can die, or you can lose touch with them. Years later, the bitterness of not forgiving will still have a hold on you; it will become a heavy burden. You will go to bed at night unable to sleep because your mind is on what that person did to you years ago. There are still people who are angry at something that happened to them forty years ago, and their family relationships suffer because they are so full of bitterness that they can't show love to anyone. Have you ever met a person like that, or, worse yet, are you that person? Are you frequently short tempered and you don't know why? Are you always defensive, feeling that people are against you? You might still be going to church, still praying, reading the Bible, but you will have no peace because you have chosen to hold onto resentment and are unwilling to forgive.

How can you forgive someone who has caused you such deep hurt? "Casting all your care upon Him, because

He cares for you" (1 Peter 5:7, NKJV). By giving it to God! It is not an easy thing to forgive, especially if someone doesn't seek forgiveness. Forgiving doesn't mean you have to let that person back in your life or even that you forget the transgressions against you. Forgiving and forgetting are two separate issues. Some believe they go hand-in-hand. But the theory that forgetting is necessary to bring about forgiveness can sometimes make forgiveness impossible. Is it reasonable to expect someone to forget a rape that makes childbearing difficult or impossible later in life? Is it reasonable to expect someone to forget a beating that leaves physical scars that you see every time you look in the mirror? I've known women who have accepted abusive men back in their lives after they and their children suffered because they believed they had to forget in order to forgive. Many preachers told them, "You must keep your family together no matter the cost," only to find that it eventually would cost them their lives. There are times we must not forget, and in fact remember, so we can keep healthy boundaries, physically, mentally, and spiritually. If we forget, we jeopardize our safety and the safety of others.

Paul says "Brethren, I do not count myself to have apprehended; but one thing I do, forgetting those things which are behind and reaching forward to those things which are ahead," (Philippians 3:13, NKJV). I believe he is saying "I'm going to let those things go. I'm dropping them, dropping those things that keep me from forging ahead, so I can move forward." So what do we do with the hurtful memories in our memory bank? I recall my own haunting childhood memories of abuse, and I remember asking God, "Please help me not to let my past hinder my present or future, but rather to let me help others to heal from the abuse they have suffered," and God answered my prayer request.

Forgiving is letting it go so God can heal you. Forgiving is not holding that charge against the person anymore and giving it to God. Sometimes, it's a daily thing: "Heavenly Father, I give this person to you. I forgive through you because I can't do it on my own, but I don't want to carry the burden anymore." Sometimes it's good to write down the pros and cons of forgiving the person, committing to paper what it will cost you to forgive and what it will cost you if you don't forgive. I believe the benefit of forgiveness far outweighs the cost of holding onto pain of not forgiving.

My girls are now twenty-seven and nineteen, and they often thank me for not putting them in the middle of our divorce. I have counseled with many people who still carry hurt because their parents used them as pawns in their divorce. I have found it is easier to go through life if you are not carrying a lot of baggage. Today when people do things that hurt me, I can choose whether I want to carry the burden of the offense or let it go. I believe I'm healthier and happier and walking in the path of holiness when I let it go. You might ask, "How can you forgive an abuser, someone who has totally done you wrong, an evil person?" You forgive them because you no longer want to be their victim. If you want to walk in victory, you have to choose not to be the victim anymore by letting the hurt go. And then the abuser is no longer a part of your life and no longer has a stronghold on you. As long as you are holding an offense against someone, they still have a stronghold on your life. "Sow for yourselves righteousness; Reap in mercy; Break up your fallow ground, For it is time to seek the Lord, Till He comes and rains righteousness on you" (Hosea 10:12, NKJV).

A fallow ground is hard ground, a land that is left uncultivated. Hosea instructs us to break up the hard places in our lives and seek the Lord 'till he comes and rains righteousness on you. A hard ground will not allow seeds to grow. Weeds don't even grow on a hard ground. Water can't even seem to soak into a hard ground. When we are unwilling to forgive and instead choose to hold onto a grudge, it becomes dirt clods in our life. Our heart becomes hard. We will get to the place where we don't trust anyone, not even God. Our heart becomes so hard that we cannot even receive the love of God.

When the arteries in your heart become clogged, you are at high risk of having a heart attack. A heart attack occurs when blood flow to a section of heart muscle becomes blocked. If the flow of blood isn't restored quickly, the section of heart muscle becomes damaged from lack of oxygen and begins to die. That is what happens to you spiritually when your heart is hardened. When bitterness builds up over many years on the inside of you, then it will bring destruction to you, causing your spirituality to slowly die. Do not allow it to germinate in the soil of your heart. When you allow your heart to harden, then it hinders the love of God from flowing through you. Ask God to show you how to soften any places in your life that have become hardened, so that the soil of your heart will be ready to receive what God has for you. Walk in mercy and see God rain his blessings upon you.

When we develop an intimate relationship with God, his character will begin to develop in you. Godliness will begin to show in you. Walk in forgiveness and love, and showing mercy will become easier. King David was a great example of someone walking in forgiveness; he was loyal to King Saul even when King Saul tried to kill him. David had to hide from King Saul, and when David had a chance to kill him, he didn't. We never see David speaking badly of King Saul or trying to hurt him in any way. David walked in mercy and forgiveness. He devoted himself to God with humility of heart. He did not allow pride to build up in him, and he did not allow hate to destroy him. David grew in godliness, and he became one of the greatest kings to ever live. He fell into sin many times, but he was quick to confess his wrongdoing and quick to repent. You will find his story in 1 and 2 Samuel. Make the choice to walk in God's holiness, so you can have peace.

When you walk in love, when you are kind to people and treat them the way you want to be treated, people will see God in you, and God will be able to rain his righteousness on you. When you wake up in the morning, be ready for God to use you. He can use you when you walk in love, and it is easier to walk in love when you have the love God in you. There are a lot of people who believe there is a God, but it's more than belief alone; you need to fall in love with God: "You shall love the Lord your God with all your heart, with all your soul, and with all your strength" (Deuteronomy 6:5, NKJV).

Facing the Death of Loved Ones

The Lord is near to those who have a broken heart,
And saves such as have a contrite spirit.

Psalm 34:18 (NKJV)

God is our refuge and strength, a very present help
in trouble.

Psalm 46:1 (nkjv)

Sometimes the difficult things appear too hard for us to attempt to resolve, so we instead choose to focus on the impossible things, the things we subconsciously know that we have no control over. When I left the doctor's office that day in April, I prayed and meditated on the quote Dr. Kwasman gave me: "Take care of the difficult things today. Leave the impossible things for tomorrow." Then I started to think on the impossible, and I asked God to help me to give it all over to him. One of the impossible things during this time was the fact that some people very close to me were dying. Of course, you or I have no control who dies and who lives, but it's only natural to wish we could have that power when the life of someone we love is involved. One of my biggest challenges has been to trust God that he knew better than I when it comes to who gets to live. "It is better to trust in the Lord than to put confidence in man. It is better to trust in the Lord than to put confidence in princes" (Psalm 118:8–9, NKJV).

Trusting God, letting him have charge over our life, is not always easy, but when we do things God's way and follow in his path, every aspect of our lives will go more smoothly. Toward the end of 2008, I had a dream, and in the dream my mother told me to take care of the things that needed to be done at home and the church, because people were going to be dying, and we, my husband and I, were going to be very busy counseling with people and arranging funerals. God has always used dreams to speak to me, so I knew this disturbing dream was a meaningful one. I woke up thinking, *How many is a lot to God?* Well, I'm still finding out.

Between December 2008 and April 2009, five people who were close to me and my family died. It was December 8, 2008, when I received a heartbreaking call that my brother only had a week to live. He had been diagnosed with brain cancer earlier in the year, but still nothing can prepare you for a call like that. I thank God that I was able to travel from Arizona to Kansas to help take care of him four different times in the last months of his life, but I knew in my heart that this time I was going home to Kansas to be with him until he died and help make sure his last days were as comfortable as possible. With cancer, as with any terminal illness, you are keenly aware that each day is a gift to be taken and cherished. We all know there are no guarantees in life, but facing that reality as you deal with a terminal illness, you truly recognize that you don't know what tomorrow will bring, so you live for the day. Not knowing what tomorrow brings makes it even more important as you face the uncertainty of each day, even each hour that you just have to put all your trust in God. "Therefore do not worry about tomorrow, for tomorrow will worry about its own things. Sufficient for the day is its own trouble" (Matthew 6:34, NKJV).

Family, friends, and the church believed for a miracle for my brother. I have seen many miracles from God, and I know that he is a God who still performs miracles. I know people who were given little time to live, and God stepped in and performed a miracle for them. Years later, they are still living. Being raised in a church that taught the faith message, we were taught to rebuke death and proclaim life; rebuke sickness and claim your healing. My family, my brother, and his church family were all proclaiming life for my brother, but my brother did not get his miracle here on earth. Instead, we saw him suffer in the end when he became unable to walk and had difficulty communicating and controlling his emotions. His friends would still come over and say, "Carl is going to live." I believe in declaring the Word of God and stating positive things, and I believe nothing is more powerful than prayer and declaring the Word of God. However, there are times when God says, "no" to our prayers and he has a better plan. That is when we have to say, "Your will be done, Lord." "'For My thoughts are not your thoughts, Nor are your ways My ways,'" says the Lord" (Isaiah 55:8, NKJV).

I believe that sometimes what people think is faith is really denial. Not wanting to face things we don't like, saying, "I don't receive that," does not mean you have faith. Sometimes, we have to receive what we believe is the bad news and say, "I am going to trust God, no matter what happens." That is faith. My sister stated that God will get no glory over our brother dying from cancer, but God is glory all by himself. God showed me that my brother was going to die and that I needed to prepare myself for it. When we deny what is happening, then we cannot prepare ourselves. Death is a part of life that we don't like to deal with, but it is still a part of life. I know people who won't get life insurance because they plan to live until the "rapture" takes place. They don't prepare for death, so when their time comes, the family is left with the financial and planning of a funeral during an already difficult time. We must face reality instead of saying, "I am not claiming that. I don't receive that," resulting in being better prepared for the inevitable life happening.

While taking care of my brother, Carl, soon after Christmas, I received a call from my oldest daughter telling me that my sister-in-law had unexpectedly passed away. She had been fine on Thursday; on Friday she got sick, and on Monday she passed away. While I could not go to her funeral, my heart grieved for her husband and her children, and I grieved knowing that any day I would face the same grief when my brother died. My brother lived four more weeks after I arrived at our sister's house where he was staying. Extended family from Tennessee, Arizona, and Kansas were able to spend what we all sadly knew would be one last Christmas with Carl. We sadly rung in the New Year together, knowing at least one certainty what the New Year would bring. We also celebrated my mother's eightieth birthday before God took my brother home on the eleventh of January.

We have the choice to look at the blessings that are in the middle of our storms and give God praise for those blessings or just focus on the storm. It truly was a blessing and a gift from God to have that time with my brother before he went on his next journey to heaven.

After returning to my home in Arizona, three people in our church whom we cared deeply for passed away. One was Sister Olga. She was the one fondly referred to as "the mother" of our church. She was the person who made everyone feel important. She was an encourager. As pastors, my husband and I recognize and value the importance of having an encourager in the church, because, unfortunately, there are always those people in the church who discourage one another. Olga was a great woman; I got even closer to her, because she was dealing with colon cancer that had spread into her liver. I visited her once a week for a couple of hours, and without fail she was always ready to encourage me, even though she was the one who was ill.

When I got back from Kansas, she was one of the first people I visited. The day I saw her she was in a lot of pain, so I convinced her to go to the hospital and took her there myself. She ended up being there for a month, and when she came home, she lived two more weeks. Her dying was a great loss both to our church and our family. She was everybody's mother. Within a short time after that, my husband lost a childhood friend as well as another of his close friends.

Being the pastors, we know we have to be strong, comfort the family, and counsel with people with little time for us to personally grieve. I miss all these people who passed away very much, but dwelling on death can certainly distract from the daily things that need to be taken care of.

Within three months of the New Year, I was tired mentally, emotionally, and physically. I felt like I had been shipwrecked. I did not have the emotional strength to offer counseling to people in the church. I was going through my own storm, deeply and silently mourning. My prayer life was very weak. I was tired and wanted to be left alone. I worried about what tomorrow would bring. I was not concerned about my health, and I stopped losing weight. I had put my life on hold. Worry gnawed at my dreams and kept me from sleeping. Oh, how my mind and body yearned for a restful night's sleep as I struggled over worrying about things that were out of my control. As humans, we can so easily slip into that worry habit. After much meditation and prayer, and after reminding myself of Dr. Kwasman's admonition to "leave the impossible for tomorrow," I realized something I had known all along—when we worry, we are taking things out of God's hands. Those hard times are when we need to trust God the most, but usually that is when we trust him least.

One day while running errands, I realized one of my daughters would soon be graduating from high school. Although I had not forgotten she was graduating, I had forgotten the usual preparations for the event coming in a matter of weeks. I had not ordered the announcements, her cap and gown, or planned a party. In fact, nothing had been done! I was thankful and relieved to learn from the school that I still had time to order everything.

It was a harsh realization to know that I had been so wrapped up in the people who died and the events of the past few months that I had not only nearly missed my daughter's important graduation milestone but also had been neglecting the people I loved the most. Yes, there is a time to grieve, but we can't let our grief rule our life and overtake us. You cannot allow grief to set up house in your life to a point that you're controlled by it. "A time to weep, and a time to laugh; A time to mourn, and a time to dance" (Ecclesiastes 3:4, NKJV).

How long should a person mourn? No one can answer that question, because it is different for everyone. However, when it is interfering with and impacting your health, or other people are getting neglected because of it, then it is time to move on to the dancing part and leave that mourning stage. The pain might stay in our heart for a long time, or even forever, but the pain will lessen as we move on. How do you just stop mourning? First, we have to make the choice to move on. It is not a bad thing to move on. Your loved one would want you to move on. They would tell you to live life to its fullest. They would say, "It's time to dance now." It's a choice you have to make. Remember that God gives us free will.

"Precious in the sight of the Lord is the death of his saints" (Psalm 116:15, NKJV). If it is precious in the sight of our Lord for a saint to go home to be with him, then it should be precious in our sight also. Now that may seem impossible, even harsh. In thinking about this concept, think of this: When I go home to Kansas to see my mother, she and the rest of my family get so excited. My nephew's wife always prepares a big dinner. My friends and family all want to know when I'm going to see them. Can you imagine how God and everyone in heaven prepare for a saint's homecoming party? God's loved one is coming home. It is a time of rejoicing in heaven. A lot of dancing and singing and rejoicing fill the heavens. God tells his people:

When you pass through the waters, I will be with you; And through the rivers, they shall not overflow you. When you walk through the fire, you shall not be burned, Nor shall the flame scorch you. For I am the Lord your God, The Holy One of Israel, your Savior.

Isaiah 43:2–3a (NKJV)

Choose to Walk in the Plan God Has for Your Life

For I know the thoughts that I think toward you,
says the Lord, thoughts of peace and not of evil, to
give you a future and a hope.

(Jeremiah 29:11, NKJV)

For I know the plans I have for you, declares the
Lord, plans to prosper you and not to harm you,
plans to give you hope and a future.

(Jeremiah 29:11, NIV)

God has a plan for everyone; he desires to give you peace, hope, and a future. We all need hope today, don't we? Jeremiah wrote a letter to the Israelites who were taken captive by Nebuchadnezzar. He let them know that they would be slaves for seventy years, and as soon as those seventy years were up, God promised to take them back home. He wanted them to know that he knew what he was doing, to be encouraged because he had a plan for them. Now I know this did not sound like a good plan, but God was telling his people: "I know the plans I have for you." There are times because of false teaching that we might believe God just thinks evil about us, that nothing good can become of our life. But God wants you to have a great future. I believe we are all created equal, and everyone has greatness inside them and in their future because we were made in the image of God. It is up to us to cultivate the greatness and do something with it. It is our choice to use what is in us to do greatness or evil.

In Genesis chapter 37–39 we read about Joseph and how God told him through a dream that he would be a leader over his brothers and father. Soon after that Joseph was being sold by his brothers as a slave. He went from dreaming of this greatness that was going to happen to him to being a slave in Egypt. He was seventeen; he knew that it was God who spoke to him, and yet it appeared to him that it could never happen now. There are times in our life when we feel a blessing is right around the corner and then all hell breaks loose on us. You may feel like you're in hell now, but that doesn't mean you have to stay there. Joseph was given favor by the man who bought him, Potiphar. Potiphar saw that the Lord was with Joseph even though he was a slave. When you are serving God, people will see God in you even when you are going through a heavy storm. Joseph was made an overseer of Potiphar's house, and then Potiphar's wife became attracted to Joseph. But Joseph did what was right in the eyes of God by not coupling with Potiphar's wife. However, she lied and said he raped her, resulting in his imprisonment. But God knew the truth (he always does!) and told him he was going to be a great leader. In spite of doing what was right, Joseph was thrown into prison. You see, life will be unfair to us, but it does not mean it will always be that way.

Joseph was a teenager and sold into slavery because he was hated by his brothers. He was taken to a foreign land where he knew no one. He was accustomed to living in wealth, and he was the spoiled child in his home. After God showed him the plans he had for him, life was no longer easy; he was going through hell. Joseph's honor was repaid with injustice, but God was still with him, even though it did not appear that way. While Joseph was in prison, God gave him favor with the prison guard. Joseph was given authority over the other prisoners, and the Lord was with him. You see, we have a choice to allow God to bless us wherever we are, or we can complain and allow depression to overtake us. Later on, Joseph was taken out of prison to interpret a dream that the Pharaoh had, and Pharaoh made him ruler over all the land of Egypt, subject only to Pharaoh. The dream that Joseph had at seventeen came to pass when he was thirty. For thirteen years Joseph had to hold on to what God showed him. Don't give up on your dreams. God did not tell Joseph at age seventeen that before he became a great leader he would first be a slave and then a prisoner. God's plan for Joseph came to pass because Joseph still served him during the time of being a slave and a prisoner. He didn't give up on God or the plan God had for him. In the end of this story, Joseph's brothers came for food, and Joseph forgave them, essentially returning good for evil. I'm sure it was a very difficult thing to do, but he did the difficult thing and God blessed him for it.

You may be going through unemployment, an illness, divorce, a lawsuit, maybe you have lost your house, but that does not mean it is the end of your story and happiness will never come your way again, even if it feels that way. It means you are about to begin another chapter in your life, and if you let God have control, then the plans that he has for you will happen. Even before you were in your mother's womb, God had a plan for you. He told Jeremiah, "Before I formed you in the womb I knew you; before you were born I sanctified you; I ordained you a prophet to the nations" (Jeremiah 1:5, NKJV).

Know this that before you were formed in your mother's womb, God had a plan for you, and it was for good and not for evil. It is for a future. He wants to give you hope today that no matter what life looks to you now, it doesn't have to remain that way. "Then you will call upon Me and go and pray to Me, and I will listen to you. And you will seek Me and find Me, when you search for Me with all your heart" (Jeremiah 29:12–13, NKJV). God wants you to find him. He is waiting for you to call on his name. He desires to be your God and your friend. You have to make the effort to call on him. He has a wonderful plan for you if you only will seek him.

Index